putt for Lower Scores

By Tony Moore and David Hutchinson

Acknowledgements

The authors would like to thank Richard Thomas (PGA Professional, Chobham Golf Club) for his help in the production of the photographs, Chobham Golf Club, Surrey, for the use of their facilities, and Neil Mountain and Dianne Moore for their considerable input.

Photographs: Chris Clark, Chris Clark Studios, Owlsmoor, Berks.
Design & Print: DC Print, Farnham, Surrey

First Edition, July 1997
Published in Great Britain by Canary Publications, a Division of Canary Ltd, registered in England number 3134103
PO Box 9, Guildford, Surrey, GU2 5GY UK
© Canary Publications, 1997

ISBN Number: 0 9531174 0 5

This book has been written to help improve the putting ability of all golfers in an attempt to improve their scores.

Are you fed up with taking too many putts on the green? Let us try to help you. This book describes a putting method that may well help you to score better. The unique practice aid supplied with this book – the Puttrite practice mat – has been devised to help you perfect your putting technique and minimise those three putts.

Like all things, practice will make perfect. However, you may find that you have some instant success if you use these principles!

How many times have you been able to reach the green in regulation only to end up with a double bogey or worse? Very often, the mid and high handicap players have poor short games; the average Club player with a low handicap often hits the ball no better than the mid handicap player – the difference is in the ability to get the ball in the hole when on and around the greens.

1. Analyse your putting performance

Total number of putts

Using the chart at the end of this book, you should analyse your putting performance over the next five rounds.

- Keep a record of the number of putts from your next five rounds (each 18 holes).

- List them in order of magnitude, lowest score at the top, highest score at the bottom of the list.

- Cross out the top and bottom scores.

- Add the three remaining scores together and then divide the total by 3.

Round	Number of Putts	Re-ordered list	Calculation
			Add up middle three scores:
1	40	36 (best score)	(a) 39
2	36	(a) 39	(b) 40
3	44	(b) 40	(c) 44
4	49	(c) 44	Sum (n): 123
5	39	49 (worst score)	Average: 123 divided by 3 = 41

If you consider two putts per hole to be regulation, on an

18 hole golf course you should score no worse than 36 putts.

If you score less than this you are already a good putter, but of

course, everyone can still improve. If you score more than

36 putts you obviously take three or more putts on some holes

– these are the holes that cost you a good score and you need

to improve!

Why do you 3-putt?

Each time you take three or more putts in your round you should note down why you did this.

- Was your approach shot to the green left some distance from the hole, leaving you a long first putt?

- Did you reach the hole or leave the putt short?

- Did you overhit the putt and leave yourself a long one back?

- Did you leave the first putt within a putter length of the hole?

- Did you misread the pace of the green?

- Did you misread any movement of the ball from right or left (break)?

- Did you misjudge the slope or nap of the green?

You may well find that you have a regular fault and this can be Improved using the methods suggested in this book.

2. Putting preliminaries

Do you have the right equipment?

There are so many different putters available to all golfers.
Indeed, you may have a really old putter handed down from
your father with a hickory shaft and traditional blade or you may
have just bought an expensive state of the art putter just like the
one used by Tiger Woods in the US Masters. You often hear the
comment that a golfer has just paid an enormous amount of
money for a new driver that he or she uses only 12 times every
round whilst selecting the ideal putter, used maybe 30 to 50
times a round, has been overlooked.

The important thing is to select a
putter that is best for you.

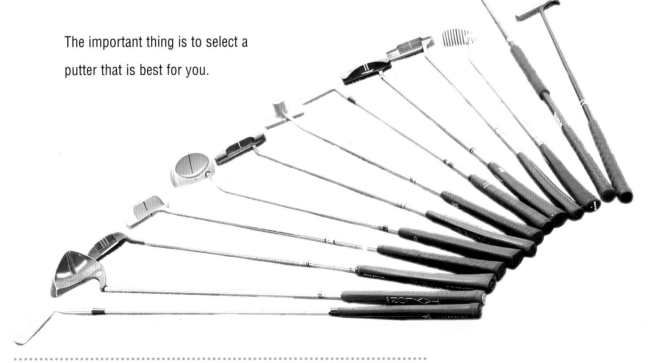

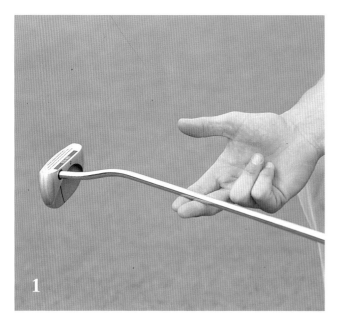 

You can test the balance of a putter by placing the index finger of your right (or left) hand on the putter's shaft towards the head of the club and balancing it so that it comes to rest in a horizontal position. If the shaft of the putter is balanced with the centre of the club, the head of the putter will point skywards (Picture 1) whilst others point toe downwards (Picture 2).

In general, you may find that a putter which balances with the face skywards, with a slightly offset shaft might be better for the mid to high handicapper; the balance of this type of putter makes it is easier to swing the clubhead backwards and forwards along a straight line.

You should also know if your putter has any loft on its face.
Some have very slight lofts as it is thought that these induce a
top-spin on the ball causing it to have a "better roll" towards
the hole.

Most putters are 35 inches long; this is an acceptable height for most people. Ladies usually prefer slightly shorter putters of say 33–34 inches in length. Putter length can be adjusted to suit your individual tastes and requirements. Many young golfers may find that a 35 inch putter is too long and their putter may need to be shortened. In general, if you have a shorter putter or grip down the shaft you may find that you have greater control and "feel" over your shot.

Finally, the grip of a putter is usually a little different to the usual club grip. It may well have a flat edge which points forwards when you take up your putting position. This enables you to place your thumbs down the shaft and helps you ensure that your hands take up the correct position of the club each time. One word of warning – if the grip is misaligned you will find it difficult to putt straight! Check that the grip is not twisted!

At the end of the day you must choose and use a putter that you like and feel confident with as well as knowing its characteristics.

Find and use the sweet spot of your putter

All putters differ slightly in the position and size of the sweet spot. This is the part of the putter face that will hit the ball best and most consistently when putting. Whichever putter you use you will need to identify the sweet spot and then try to align this point on the putter face with the centre of the ball, each time you address it.

Place the putter on the ground in front of you, as if you were going to make a putt. Grip the putter at the bottom of the grip with the thumb and index finger of the right hand only. Next, raise the putter in the air so that it hangs to the ground (Picture 3). Take a coin in the left hand and tap the face of the putter, starting at the heel and moving towards the toe (Picture 4). You will find a point (near the centre) when the putter moves backwards in a straight line without twisting; this is the "sweet spot". Mark this place (for example on the top edge of the putter) with a felt pen. As you carry on moving towards the toe, away from the sweet spot, the putter will start to twist again as you tap it.

Some putters have the sweet spot already marked – this may be the incorrect place so check it anyway.

3

You should always try to hit the ball with the sweet spot of the putter.

4

5

6a ✗

6b ✔

3. Improve your putting technique

The aim of putting is to "sink the putt"! You are more likely to do this if you are able to impart an over–spin on the ball. You can test to see how you hit the ball as follows:

Place a golf ball in the plastic template provided. The ball should just go in half way if it is the correct size (if the ball is too small it is illegal!). Draw a line around the centre of the ball using a fairly thick permanent marker, remove the ball and let it dry (Picture 5). Alternatively, you could use a ball which has each half as a different colour.

Align the ball so that the centre line is perpendicular to the putter face, pointing in the direction of travel. Hit your putt. If you are imparting cut–spin on the ball, because you are hitting it badly, the line will disappear or become blurred when it travels along the ground (Picture 6a). If you are hitting the ball properly the line will be clearly visible all the time as it rolls with only over–spln (Picture 6b).

By using the putting technique in the following sections you should be able to improve the "strike quality" of your putts leading to better scores.

Step 1: Gripping the putter

Hold the putter in front of you with the head touching the
ground and the face of the putter pointing towards the direction
you want to hit the ball. Place the palms of each hand perfectly
square to the face of the putter, either side of the grip, then grip
the putter with a conventional overlap grip, making sure that
your thumbs are pointing directly down the grip of the putter
(Pictures 7 and 8). Any twist of the hands at this point might
lead to you taking the putter away on an incorrect line.

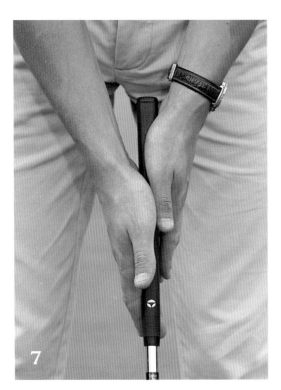
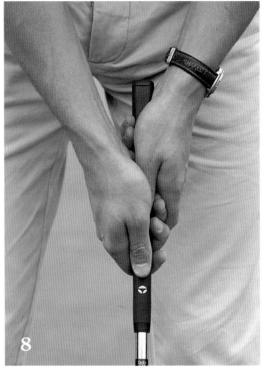

Step 2: Take up your Stance

Initially, take up a stance so that a line drawn from your toes points towards the hole. Your feet should be about two feet apart (not too wide, not too narrow). The ball should be positioned towards the front of your stance (Picture 9).

Next move the left foot backwards slightly and then position the putter, using the grip described in Step 1, behind the ball so that it rests lightly on the ground (try not to press the putter into the ground as this makes the take away more difficult). Check that the right foot is lined up square to the hole (Picture 10).

Step 3: Make sure that your eyes are over the ball

Make sure your eyes are over the ball (Picture 11) .

Do this by modifying your feet position, and by moving the head backwards or forwards to obtain a comfortable position in relation to the ball. Your weight should be balanced on the sole of your feet, neither too much on the heels or the toes.

You can now use the special Puttrite practice mat and ball size disk included with this book to check that your eyes are over the ball.

- Place the Puttrite practice mat on the ground in front of you so that the red section is furthest away from you.

- If you are right handed, place the ball size disk alongside the Puttrite practice mat as shown (if you are left handed, turn the mat around and put the disk at the opposite end of the mat). You will need a golf ball to test your eye position.

- Lay your putter behind the ball on the black mark.

- Take up your normal putting position.

- To check if your eyes are "over the ball", drop a golf ball from the bridge of your nose and see if it lands on the ball

size disk. If it does not you need to adjust your position until the ball drops directly from your eyes and lands on the ball size disk on the ground. (Adjustments can be made by moving your feet and head; gripping down the putter will also adjust your eye position). You should avoid simply leaning forwards so that you are overbalanced. Alternatively, you could use a mirror in place of the disk to see if your eyes are visible when you take up your stance (you do not need to drop the ball!)

- When putting, it is best if your eyes are directly over the ball (but not beyond it!). Try to memorise this putting position and use it every time you putt. Check your eye position on a regular basis using this method.

Step 4: Think about your take away: avoid a "wristy flick"

Try to immobilise the lower part of your body. Your shoulders and arms should pivot to make the putting stroke. Try to avoid using your wrists in the action as this will cause the ball to be flicked left or right! Excessive body movement coupled with a wristy flick will give rise to a disastrous putting action.

Keep the wrists firm and loosen the shoulders.

Before you putt, relax the arms. You can try squeezing the grip quite hard a couple of times and then relaxing the muscles in an attempt to relieve the tension in those "pressure putt" situations. Another tip is to apply pressure on the middle joint of the index finger of the right hand using the thumb when gripping the club – this has the effect of "locking" the right wrist (if you are left handed, for right hand read left hand and vice versa).

Step 5: Take the putter away along the best path to generate a good roll

If you are right handed push the putter away to the right using the left hand to dominate this action. Keep the wrist of the left hand firm as you do this. This is really important – make it one of your "swing thoughts". By keeping the wrist of the left hand firm during the putting stroke you will prevent your wrists becoming active and "flicking" at the ball.

Keep wrist
firm to
prevent
"flicking" at
the ball

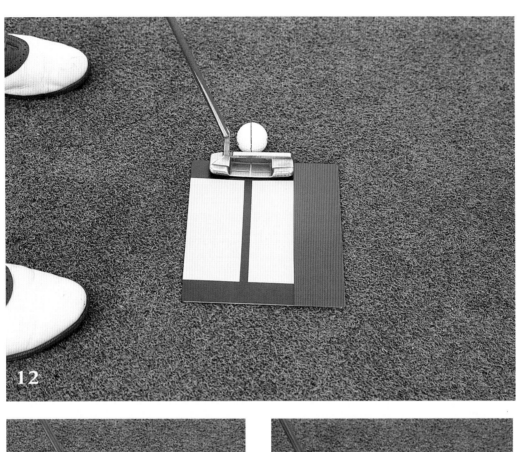

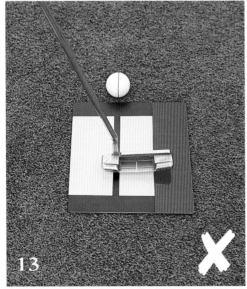

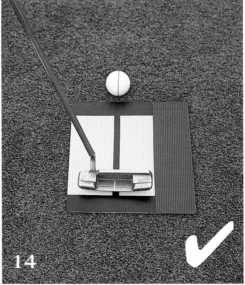

If you are left handed . . .

push the putter away to the left using the right hand.

Keep the wrist of the right hand firm as you do this.

This is really important – make this one of your "swing thoughts". By keeping the wrist of the right hand firm during the putting stroke you will prevent your wrists becoming active and "flicking" at the ball.

You should try to ensure that the toe of the putter always stays in the yellow section of the pad, NEVER THE RED SECTION (Pictures 12, 13 and 14). This will ensure that the putter is taken away straight back or slightly inside the line. The black line on the Puttrite practice mat will help you achieve this.

If the toe of the putter ever goes into the red section you are taking the putter outside the line and this will cause the ball to move and oscillate toward the hole with cut–spin, leading to missed putts often due to "lipping out".

A word of warning –

Try to keep your eyes on the ball when striking it – avoid lifting your head too soon to watch where it has gone or how it is rolling.

Use the ball with the line around its centre to see if the ball is rolling without cut–spin. Practice hitting the ball using this technique until you consistently take the putter away correctly and hit the ball without oscillation and cut–spin. Top–spin or over–spin forces the ball downwards into the hole. Hitting the ball when the putter head is taken back slightly inside the line helps develop over–spin. Cut–spin causes the ball to spin parallel to the surface of the green making it less likely to drop into the hole (Picture 15).

15

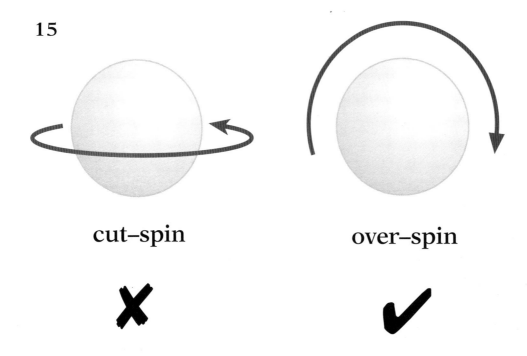

cut–spin   over–spin

4. Selecting the right line and length

Putting is really simple if you are able to do two things:

1. Hit the ball along the correct line to the hole. Often this involves judging how much the ball will break from right to left or left to right and also having the ability to identify the straight putt.

2. Hit the ball at the right pace to hole the putt. You can choose to hit the ball hard, thus minimising any break that there may be, or you can hit the ball with exactly the right amount of pace to reach the hole and perhaps go only a few inches past if you miss.

How to judge the line

This is one of the most difficult things to do when putting. Experience gained when playing the same course many times will help you here; try to remember what happened to your putts from different parts of the green – or even better, make a drawing of the green and mark on it how the ball breaks (like caddies do for the tournament players).

Some of the following guidelines can help you to judge the line of the putt:

- Crouch down behind your ball, about 3 paces away. Look along the path of your ball to the hole. Try to determine if the ground slopes from right to left, left to right or indeed, both directions (Picture 16).

- You need to visualise how the ball will travel when you hit it. Plot out an imaginary path that you must follow. Experience will tell you how far up a hill you need to hit the ball.
  Remember though – the harder you hit the ball the more it will follow a straight path and less the influence of slopes.

16

- The ball will break less on a slow green where the grass is quite long. On the other hand, on fast "slick" greens (with very short grass), it will break much more. For all putts, when the ball slows down it will break more.

- In some countries (like Florida in the USA) the green has a nap. This is because the thick bladed grass (Bermuda grass) grows towards the sun and lays at an angle on the green. If you hit into the nap, the ball travels slower and is less susceptible to break. A ball hit with the nap could break more.

- Use the cut lines or other natural markings, such as old pitch marks, leaves or different shades of grass on the green. These can help you plot your line to the hole. However, you cannot place any item on the green to help you identify your line!

- Look at the sides of the hole. If the hole is cut on a slope you will notice that one side of the hole from the surface to the rim of the cup is deeper than the other side. The ball is likely to break from the deepest part of the hole.

- Remember that the slower the ball is moving the more it is likely to break. When the putt is first hit, the ball is moving faster and the early slopes therefore have less effect than at the end of the path of the putt when the ball is moving slower.

- Once you have identified the path of your ball, choose a point midway along the line (midpoint marker) and then another point about one foot in front of your ball along the way to the midpoint marker (line marker point). Aim your putt so that your ball travels over the "line marker point" (Picture 17).

- It is better to overestimate break rather than underestimate it – miss on the professional side rather than the low side for amateurs! There is always a chance that a ball may drop in through the side door if you are too high – this never happens if you underestimate the break.

Your only remaining decision is how hard to hit the ball.

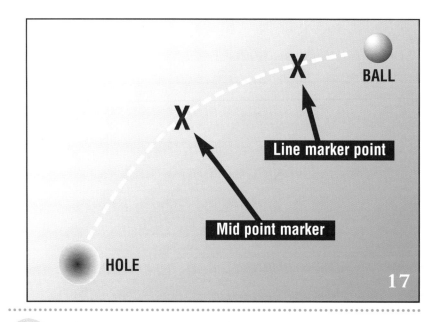

How to judge the pace

In professional tournaments the pace of a green is regulated and measured using a stimp meter. This is simply a method of rolling a ball down a fixed slope on to the green and measuring how far it travels. The higher the stimp reading, the greater the distance travelled and hence the faster the green. Amateur golfers are not lucky enough to be told how fast the green is in usual circumstances and they have to rely totally on their own judgment. Some of the following factors will help you to judge how hard to hit a putt.

- The ball you are using will determine how hard you have to hit the ball. A three-piece soft covered ball with a wound centre, like a balata ball, will need to be hit much harder than, for example, a two piece ball that has a solid centre and a more durable cover.

- You must decide how fast the green is. In general, greens with long grass that are quite green in colour will be slower than one that is closely mown. If the grass is growing towards you the putt will be slower than if you are putting with the nap.

- Sand, top dressing and water on a green make it slower. Holes caused by hollow-tining also tend to slow the ball down. If the green has just been watered or it is raining, hit the ball harder. On the otherhand, ice and frost may well speed up the green and in some cases water may cause an overhit putt to aquaplane making it fly past the hole.

- Greens on links courses tend to be faster as they consist of narrow bladed grasses (eg fescue grass). The green often looks brown on top. Usually they are sand based and the wind off the sea dries the surface. On parkland courses the greens tend to be slower as the grass may be broad bladed (rye grasses).

- All greens tend to be faster after they have been cut. In the late afternoon, when there has been a whole day's growth, greens tend to be slower. In some parts of the world, for example Florida, you can almost see the grass growing and at the end of the day the greens are distinctly slower.

- Wind can affect a putt. If you are putting into the wind hit it harder, and softer if you are downwind. Strong winds can also affect the line of the putt.

- Slow greens require a much firmer stroke. The technique suggested in this book will help you get a good roll on the ball and this will help you on slow greens. Really fast greens require little more than a gentle tap with the putter.

- You need to check whether you have an uphill or downhill putt. It is no use overhitting a downhill putt as you will go way past the hole. If you are uphill you need to hit the ball harder.

- Always try to go past the hole. If you miss, watch what happens to the ball as it goes by the hole to see if there is any break.

- If you intend to hit the ball at the hole to avoid break, more pace is required than if you are aiming to reach the hole and use the break of the green.

18

- If you have a long putt and have decided to get the ball close (laying up), try to imagine a circle around the hole about the size of a car tyre. Imagine that this is the hole and plan to hit the ball into this circle (Picture 18). This makes your second putt much easier!

- Do not assume that every green on the same course will be the same pace. Often they are not. You must consider the pace of every single putt carefully, not taking too much time as this will annoy your playing partners and others.

- To judge pace, when crouching behind the ball to judge the line, it might help you to imagine that a small car (the ball) is making its way to the hole – try to visualise how it gets there (that is the line) and also how much energy it needs to reach the hole – plenty of energy to go uphill and virtually freewheeling downhill. If you have to putt over the brow of a "hill", judge the energy needed to just take it to the top of the hill, letting it freewheel downhill.

- Watch the pace of the putts of your playing partners. You might learn about line and length from them.

19a 19b 19c

- You should learn to judge the pace of a putt on a practice
  putting green. Place a golf tee about 10, 20 and
  30 centimetres behind your ball, just outside the line of the
  backswing. Take the putter away so that you go level with
  the first tee – see how far the ball goes. Try it with the
  second and third tees (Pictures 19a, 19b and 19c). This will
  give you some idea how far back to take your putter to
  achieve certain distances. Then with your basic knowledge,
  adjust the length of your backswing to adapt to the different
  conditions and greens on the course.

• Another technique to help you determine how hard to hit a putt is as follows. For a short putt, take up a narrow stance, place the ball towards the front of your stance and take the putter away until it reaches the big toe of your right foot (or left foot if you are left handed) (Picture 20a). For a longer putt, widen your stance slightly and again take the putter away until it reaches the big toe of your right foot; the longer the backswing the further the ball will travel (Picture 20b). This is a good drill for the practice green; you might also want to try it on the course!

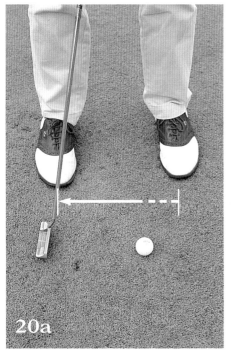

20a

20b

Tip for "putts" when the ball is just off the green

If the ball comes to rest just off the green, for example,

on the fringe, the grass tends to be slightly longer

making it more difficult to judge the pace of your putt.

One way to play this shot is to putt the ball as if you were

on the green itself but deliberately hit above the centre of the

ball so that you impart top–spin on it. This will generate a

better roll of the ball towards the hole (making it travel further

than normal) and this compensates for the longer grass,

allowing you to plan the pace of the putt as if you were on the

green itself.

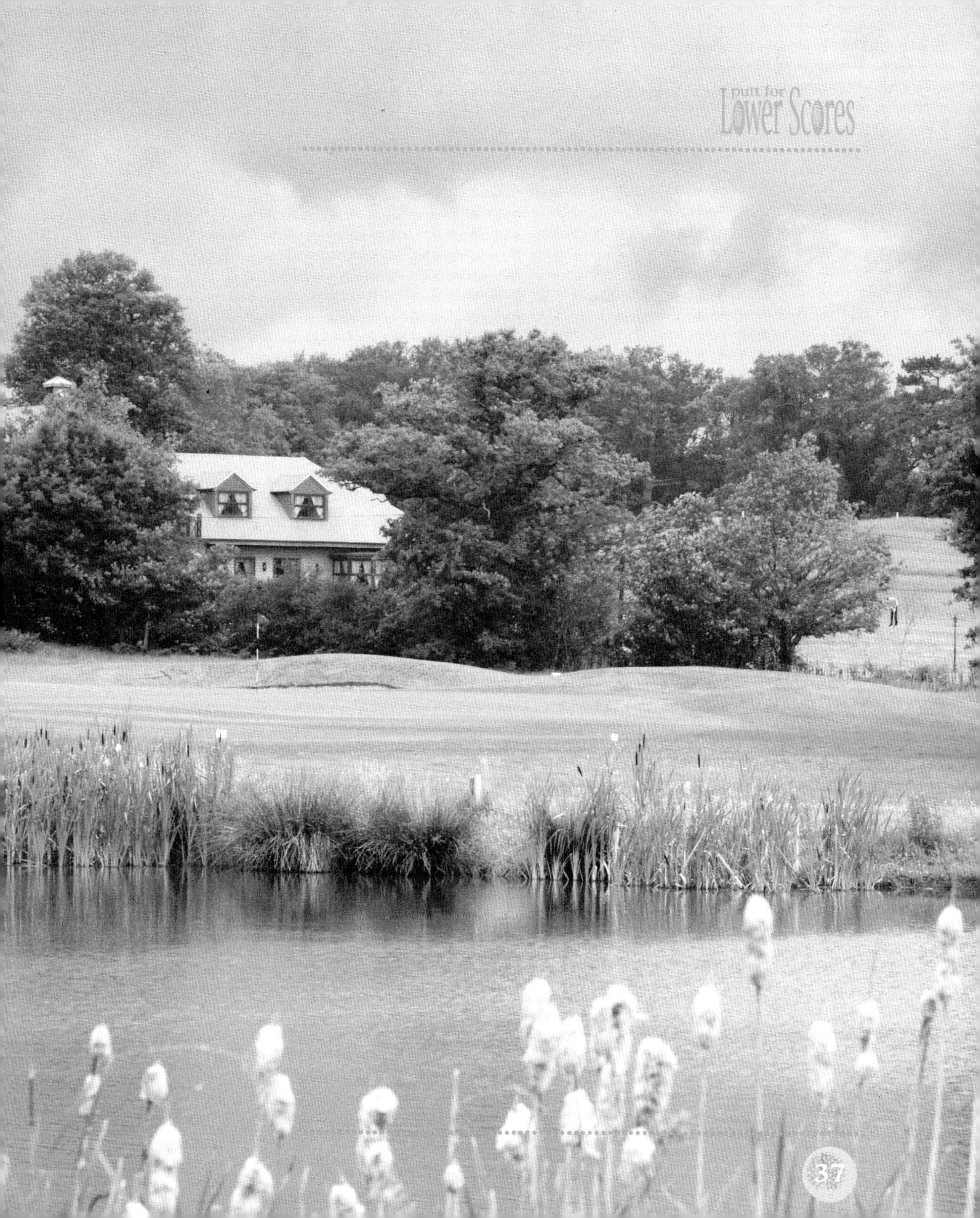

5. Positive mental attitude

Putting can be a real pleasure – you should enjoy trying to make a putt and not be frightened of it. Words like can't, won't, and don't are banned! You will do better if you have a positive attitude towards putting. Never say to your partner " I am not putting well, I don't think I can hole anything today"! You must always believe that you can and will hole every putt that you make. Enjoy putting, try not to be nervous and tense over putts, this is only the start to having an imaginary golf disease called the "yips"!

> **You must believe that you can hole every putt.**
> **Then go ahead and do it.**

If you have a difficult putt to make, take a deep breath and quickly expire. When taking stance, grip the putter tightly for a few seconds and relax the grip. Do this a few times. This helps you to relax the muscles in the forearm. Tension is the cause of many missed putts.

6. A practice drill before you go out on the course

Try to avoid going on to the first tee without having had a practice putt! The following simple drill on the practice putting green will help you "tune in" your putting stroke.

Take four balls on to the green. Select a hole that is fairly flat. Try to hole putts about 2 feet away (very simple!), and then increase the distance, hitting four balls each time: 3 feet, 5 feet, 8 feet, 12 feet and then finish off with a few very long putts, trying to get them up to the hole. If you are a mid handicap golfer, you should expect to hole all of the short putts up to say 3 feet – if you do not, go back to basics and check your putting technique. You should hole one or two of the mid range putts and if you hole a long one – well done!

Finish off with a few more short putts to build your confidence.

7. Putting etiquette

- When walking on to the green look for your pitch mark and repair it. Unrepaired pitch marks cause serious damage to the putting surface and you may suffer from poor greens at a later date.

- Place a marker directly behind your ball before partner or opponent plays – you should use a flat marker if in line. Never use a golf tee that penetrates the green – against the rules and you will incur a penalty! Replace the ball immediately in front of the marker (Picture 21).

- Walk around golf balls (and markers) on the green, do not tread on yours or someone else's line. Avoid walking on the area near the hole; remember also to avoid the area through the line of your and your opponents' putts as you do not wish to damage an area that may have to be putted over later. Avoid putting out if you will stand on or near someone else's line because it may "spike-up" or compress the green near the hole.

- Stand quiet and still: motion or noise is distracting. Never put your hands in pocket and jingle coins, sneeze, blow nose, fiddle with golf bags etc. Distracting an opponent at any time is socially unacceptable and you will win no friends if you do this!

- Attend the flag by standing to one side (so that no shadow is over the hole or down the line), hold the top of the flag (preventing the flag itself flapping in the wind), hold the flagpole at near arms length, upright in the hole, and stand still until the putt is made (Picture 22). As the ball rolls towards the hole, remove the flag and carefully place it on the ground well away from the hole. Do not throw the flag down as it may cause damage to the putting green.

22

- Sometimes you might have to move your marker if it is on someone else's line. To do this, pick a fixed point in the distance at 90 degrees to line of the ball's path to the hole. Use the blade of your putter to move the marker towards the distant point until it is out of the way (Picture 23). Remember to reverse this process so that you replace your ball where it originally was.

- You can check your line and estimate pace whilst others are planning their putts. Do not wait until it is your turn.

- You may stand behind your ball. If someone else has the same line however, do not stand directly behind them but discreetly to one side so as not to distract. Do not stand in the line of the putt.

- Place your golf bag away from the putting surface, to the back edge of the green near to where you intend to exit to go to next hole. Do not waste time and hold others up by leaving your bag at the front of the green.

23

- Furthest from the hole putts in usual play. If someone is still off the green, but nearer to the hole than someone on the green, that player is often allowed to play up but there is no fixed ruling on this. Talk to your partners to determine an acceptable order of play on every hole.

- In match play, the team furthest from the hole may nominate which team member putts first (even if they are nearest to the hole) – this can be used tactically to get a score on the card and then allow the team mate a "free shot" to try to better the score. This is a socially acceptable tactic in match play at all levels.

- You may elect to putt out in stroke play but **not** in match play, unless you are furthest from the hole.

- Replace the flag firmly in the hole – if you do not it can lean over and damage the edge of the hole. Make sure someone puts the flag back in – in general each player does his or her share of this during the round!

8.   Putting performance charts

You may photocopy these charts and use them to calculate your putting average, before trying our system and then at regular intervals afterwards.

You should play the same course each time.

Date:

Round	Number of Putts	Re-ordered list	Calculation
			Add up middle three scores:
1		(best score)	(a)
2		(a)	(b)
3		(b)	(c)
4		(c)	Sum: (n)
5		(worst score)	Average: (n) divided by 3 =

Date:

Round	Number of Putts	Re-ordered list	Calculation
			Add up middle three scorcs:
1		(best score)	(a)
2		(a)	(b)
3		(b)	(c)
4		(c)	Sum: (n)
5		(worst score)	Average: (n) divided by 3 =

Date:

Round	Number of Putts	Re-ordered list	Calculation
			Add up middle three scores:
1		(best score)	(a)
2		(a)	(b)
3		(b)	(c)
4		(c)	Sum: (n)
5		(worst score)	Average: (n) divided by 3 =

Date:

Round	Number of Putts	Re-ordered list	Calculation
			Add up middle three scores:
1		(best score)	(a)
2		(a)	(b)
3		(b)	(c)
4		(c)	Sum: (n)
5		(worst score)	Average: (n) divided by 3 =

Date:

Round	Number of Putts	Re-ordered list	Calculation
			Add up middle three scores:
1		(best score)	(a)
2		(a)	(b)
3		(b)	(c)
4		(c)	Sum: (n)
5		(worst score)	Average: (n) divided by 3 =